PEOPLE ARE
awesome

kindness
is free.

sprinkle
that stuff
everywhere.

PEOPLE ARE
awesome

everyday acts of kindness that will
restore your faith in humanity

emma hill

introduction

We live in increasingly troubled times defined by cyber bullying, climate change, self-serving politicians and a media that peddels vitriol. But there is hope in the backlash that is the rise of the cult of kindness. People are increasingly realizing that for a harmonious world, all we really need to do is be kind to one another.

Showing kindness to others has a huge array of benefits. It reduces stress and anxiety, releases feel-good hormones, and can improve energy and overall happiness. Kindness is also contagious; when someone is on the receiving end of it, they are significantly more likely to pay it forwards.

In this book you will find stories of kindness that will inspire you to share the love in your everyday life. Whether it's a big, small, unnoticed or simple act of kindness, remember – one person being awesome is all it takes to change the world.

the shoes
off his feet

A New York City subway passenger captured on camera the moment a stranger gave a homeless man his shoes. As temperatures dipped close to freezing, the man said he noticed that the homeless man had tattered shoes with holes in them; he was worried for him given the freezing temperatures. "I only had two blocks to walk home from the subway station," he continued, "I did that in my socks. I have a warm apartment to go home to – not everyone has that kind of privilege."

real-life santa

Capturing the true spirit of Christmas, an anonymous benefactor posted envelopes of cash through people's letterboxes over the festive season in a random act of kindness to spread some Christmas cheer. Families in a West London suburb reported that wads of cash had been delivered through their door, slipped into a card with a note wishing them a wonderful Christmas. "It has totally changed our Christmas," one recipient reported. "We have been able to buy the children the presents they were hoping for and invite relatives to join us for a big family dinner, something we would never have been able to afford without this act of kindness."

retrieved keys

A man returned to his car in a supermarket car park only to discover that he had locked his keys and phone inside. A 17-year-old boy working as a trolley attendant noticed the man's distress and, upon learning what had happened, cycled the 10-mile round trip to the man's house to collect the spare keys from his wife. "I needed the exercise," he claimed.

a little
helping hand

A proud grandma reported how her 5-year-old granddaughter's thoughtfulness made her heart swell. When playing in their local park with some other children, she stopped a little boy who had joined in with their games, knelt down and tied his shoelaces having just learnt to tie her own. "This little moment of kindness filled me with pride!" she declared.

the fairy godmother

A mother was browsing with her daughter for a prom dress, struggling to find one she could afford. In a particular shop there was a sale rail with some discounted items and, amazingly, her daughter had selected one of these dresses – it fitted perfectly and she looked beautiful in it. Taking it to the cashier they discovered that the dress was not in the sale after all. They left disappointed, but a few minutes later a stranger tapped the mother on the arm and handed over a bag – with the dream dress inside. "I couldn't help overhearing your conversation," she said, "and I just wanted to buy the dress for your daughter."

floral
delivery

A retired horticulturalist plants the seeds of kindness in her neighbourhood by delivering beautiful home-grown blooms to her neighbours every Friday. "Her garden is absolutely stunning," said one happy recipient. "To be gifted some of its gems makes our week. Knowing we have fresh flowers to brighten up the house all weekend is really special. Even in winter she manages to make up attractive bouquets of evergreens and berries."

neighbours
in need

Whilst many supermarket shelves were emptied during the coronavirus pandemic, one 10-year-old boy took it upon himself to do some stockpiling of his own. He spent his pocket money on essential goods that elderly people living on his road were finding hard to get hold of – such as pasta and toilet rolls. He then knocked on doors and delivered the care packages. "He just asked me to take him to the local shop and bought all this stuff out of his own pocket," said his mother.

hidden money

A bookstore browser got more than she bargained for when she opened a book in which she found £20 and a note saying "Hi, wishing you an awesome day today. The world is smiling on you. Enjoy a cup of coffee on me, or pass it on to make someone else smile." To pay it forward she bought coffee and sandwiches and gave them out to the homeless people she passes on her way to work

strength in numbers

A crowd of 100 London commuters helped lift a bus to free a cyclist trapped beneath it. Footage on social media showed passersby stopping and coming together to help. The cyclist spent a month recovering in hospital and was moved to tears watching the footage of his rescue.

food for
a family

One family recalled how when going through a particularly tough time with divorce, redundancy and mounting bills, they would find boxes of food on their doorstep every morning. This continued for months, until the mother found a new job. They never found out who was dropping off the parcels.

a bed for
the night

A couple paid for 80 hotel rooms for homeless people in Chicago during the depths of winter. This act of compassion also stretched to arranging for pizzas to be delivered and their clothes to be laundered.

letters for the lonely

One 14-year-old boy has started his very own chain of kindness. He visits elderly people in his village in England, helping them with odd jobs such as mowing their lawns. Seeing how lonely some of the older residents of the village were inspired him to take his kindness a step further and he set up a scheme at his school, with the support of his head teacher, that involves pupils writing letters to the more isolated villagers.

flowerbombing the city

One resident spreads joy every spring by scattering wild flowers on wastelands around her home city, planting flowers on empty land, and placing hanging baskets and pots of flowers along the most derelict of streets. She has become infamous among residents of the city, known simply as "the flower lady".

gift for
a teacher

A schoolteacher from Ohio once received a surprise gift from one of her pupils. Inside her workbook the schoolgirl had hidden an envelope in which she'd placed her $20 birthday money and a note saying that she had decided teachers didn't get paid enough so she wanted to give her this money. "I of course had to decline the touching gesture," the teacher said, "but I was so moved and her thoughtfulness brought tears to my eyes."

free
rides

In honour of the friend he lost to drink-driving, a 25-year-old man would frequent the busiest part of the town on weekends, offering free rides to groups of people who had been drinking, in order to keep the roads safe. His altruism caught on, and friends and acquaintances were soon offering to help him out and work shifts. "I let people play their own music," he says, "and so far nobody has thrown up in my car."

kangaroo care

A policeman went above and beyond the call of duty when he rescued a baby kangaroo from the side of the road in Western Australia. It had been hit by a car and was severely malnourished and dehydrated. He took the animal home and nursed it back to full health for 18 months.

parking paid

An elderly man was full of praise for a young stranger who lent a hand whilst he was trying to pay for his parking. The machine wouldn't accept his note, and with a big line forming behind him, he was getting flustered. Then a young boy of 18 came along and popped the correct change in the machine for him. "That small moment restored my faith in humanity," the old man declared.

a doorstep concert

In troubled times, a little music goes a long way in soothing the soul and lifting spirits. Two talented siblings spread the power of music during the coronavirus pandemic by putting on concerts for their neighbour who was self-isolating and unable to leave the house. The pair broke out their cellos and played her favourite classical music pieces on her porch. "They brought light into those dark days," she said.

department
of kindness

A department of kindness has been opened at a Bristol maternity hospital to celebrate kindness and promote the wellbeing of staff. A local artist runs creative making sessions to enable staff to slow down and take a little time out for themselves. Staff are encouraged to drop in and take part in simple creative activities such as collages. "As a health professional, you have to have a constant kindness output – but what about the kindness input?" Brown asked. Midwives are appreciating the time away from the wards to slow down and de-stress.

a sweet moment

A woman who works in a clothes shop recalls the time she exchanged pleasantries with a customer, a young woman around the same age as her. "It was a busy day and I was tired, stressed and more than a little grumpy," she remembers. "I joked to her that it was nothing a bar of chocolate wouldn't solve." A short time later the customer returned with a big bar of chocolate for the sales assistant. "I'll never forget that simple yet powerful gesture of kindness. It was a small thing, but it made me feel great."

lunch
for ten

A man travelling on a bus noticed a homeless man wandering up to the driver looking for food. The bus driver handed over a sandwich, fruit and water. When he got off the bus, the passenger asked the driver why he was so willing to hand over his lunch like that, only to be told that the driver packs ten lunches a day so he can hand them out to those in need.

coupon collection

A tech-savvy teen spent weeks scouring websites and seeking out special offers so he could buy items to donate to families at Christmas. He managed to collect £800 worth of shopping coupons and spent them on toys, electrical goods, clothing and household items, which he donated to a charity that delivers goods to those in need.

an open door

A café on the Greek island of Lesbos opens its doors to stray dogs during cold nights. The owner is keen to provide them with a warm, safe place to stay "so they won't freeze to death outside." Once the customers leave, the dogs are welcomed in.

a stranger pays for shopping

A young mum was full of gratitide when a stranger stepped in to pay for her shopping. She had a week's worth of groceries piled up and packed only to discover she had lost her bank card. "I felt so stressed," she said. "The queue was building up and I heard someone tutting and my baby was getting unsettled." The man behind her stepped up and paid for her shopping. "It was no bother, I had enough money on me," her humble saviour claimed.

caring for the carers

One woman in New Jersey felt compelled to help the medical workers in her community during the coronavirus pandemic. They were becoming more stretched and working longer hours as more cases were confirmed. Meanwhile, local restaurants were struggling to stay in business during lockdown. She came up with an idea that would help both parties – she wrote a Facebook post asking friends if they would donate money to be spent at local restaurants on food that would then be delivered to the hardworking medical staff. The response was overwhelming and her team was able to deliver lunches and late evening dinners to the hospital on a daily basis.

sharing
sandwiches

A woman left a café about to tuck into her longed-for warm sandwich on a cold day when she noticed a homeless man sitting at the bus stop. Realizing he was far more in need than her, she felt compelled to offer him her sandwich. Another customer leaving the sandwich shop had observed this exchange and promptly gave the kind woman half of her sandwich.

kindness leading to friendship

One fateful day, a 25-year-old woman was travelling on a train back to London when a ticket inspector came to check tickets. The woman rummaged through her bag in increasing desperation, and realized she had lost both her ticket and her wallet. Another woman in the same carriage overheard and paid for her ticket. They got chatting and on alighting the train went for a drink together. Twenty years later they are still friends.

a sweet exchange

Whilst eating at their local diner, a retired couple discovered that due to financial restraints their waitress walked a 16-mile round trip to get to work. Always cheerful and always ready to give her customers an extra scoop of ice cream, the couple was determined to help her. So one day they left an extremely generous tip. When they paid their bill, they also left a set of car keys. Racing after them the waitress told them they'd left their car keys behind, only to be told they were in fact her car keys and that they'd bought her a car.

vending
machine treat

One man has got into the habit of taping envelopes full of change to vending machines so the next visitor can enjoy a sweet treat on him. One happy recipient reports finding the envelope and a note saying "Enjoy a sweet treat on me. Pass it on!" So she used the money to buy her snack then left change for the next person, paying the kindness forward.

love for
stray dogs

A 9-year-old boy from the Philippines spent all of his pocket money on dog food to feed the stray dogs in his neighbourhood. His story went viral and donations flooded in from all over the world. These enabled him to realize his dream of setting up an animal shelter to rescue stray cats and dogs, feed and care for them, and rehome them wherever possible.

giving your all

One homeless man's gesture in the Northern England city of Preston meant more than most. A student was stranded late at night, and he gave her his last £3 so she could get a taxi home. Overwhelmingly touched by this gesture, the student organized a sleep-out to raise money so the homeless man could put a deposit on a flat. She raised over £12,500, which enabled him to get off the streets and into permanent accommodation.

flying solo

A young mother recounts how her baby was screaming and her 3-year-old was having a tantrum over a colouring book when they were boarding their flight. She recalls feeling mortified and awful for whoever was going to be sat next to them – she was sure they would ask to be moved. Whilst struggling to get her daughter strapped in, a nearby passenger and grandmother swooped in and scooped the baby up, comforting him and soothing him and offering words of encouragement to the mother. Once they were all settled, the grandma played games with the daughter, drew pictures with her and engaged her in conversation. "Never have I been so grateful for the kindness of a stranger," the mother said.

a generous tip

A student working in a coffee shop was chatting with a co-worker about how they didn't have enough money for the bus ride home and started joking about ways they could pull in better tips! A customer overheard them and came back half an hour later with annual bus passes for them both.

cleaning
the streets

Transforming the reputation of teenagers in their hometown is a group of students who decided to start cleaning up their town centre. Every Saturday afternoon they gather to litter pick. Their group is ever growing and attracts admiration from residents and businesses alike.

caring for cats

A nurse in Peru swaps her day job for another caring role when she gets home after her shifts – she tends to nearly 200 sick cats, having turned her home into a sanctuary for them. The mother of three has been running the cat hospice for many years and pays for their care with a combination of her own money and donations she receives for their food and medicine.

hug on a hard day

One day a woman was having a particularly challenging shopping trip with her autistic son. "At the checkout my son was getting louder and louder as his frustration built over not being able to voice what he wanted," she recalls. "A lady in front of us turned around and shouted at him to keep the noise down. I was so upset I bundled us both out of the shop as quickly as possible. As I was putting the shopping in the car, tears streaming down my face, a woman who had been in the shop came over and gave me a big hug. I can't put into words how much that hug meant to me and I will never forget it."

milk and so much more

During the coronavirus pandemic one milkman worked around the clock to care for the most vulnerable people in his area. He delivered food parcels to his self-isolating customers and has been known to pick up prescriptions, mow lawns and share books.

shaving heads in solidarity

A 10-year-old schoolgirl was anxious about returning to school after receiving cancer treatment that resulted in hair loss. Her best friend, who she'd confided in, decided to shave her head in an act of solidarity. This inspired dozens of other students, and even the teachers, to do the same. The school took the opportunity to turn this great act of kindness into a fundraising event and raised thousands of pounds for a childhood cancer charity.

treasure hunt

A 6-year-old girl and her mother decided to spread a little kindness around their neighbourhood with a packet of chalks and handfuls of little gifts. They chalked up colourful arrows on the pavement to guide people towards hiding spots where the treasures could be found. "We hung around and watched a few of the presents being found," said the mother. "Seeing the delighted faces was a total joy."

setting a positive example

A woman who notified her team that she was taking some time off to focus on her mental health received plaudits from her boss. The CEO of the company replied to her candid email telling her "You are an example to us all, and help cut through the stigma so we can all bring our whole selves to work."

postcard campaign

A freelance copywriter came up with a way to help combat loneliness during the coronavirus lockdown – a postcard scheme that enabled vulnerable members of society to easily request help from their neighbours. She designed the postcard, which enabled recipients to ask for help with shopping, collecting medical supplies, or a simple chat on the phone, and posted it on Facebook so people could download it and deliver it through their neighbours' doors. This scheme, and many others like it, became part of a coronavirus "caremongering" movement that spread through towns, cities, villages and countries around the world as people came together to help one another in times of need.

cashier pays

A cashier attempted to pull off a discreet act of kindness when he helped a customer in need, but his good deed was captured on camera and went viral. The credit card of one of the elderly regulars in his store kept getting declined. So the cashier quietly paid with his own money and didn't mention it. The customer assumed his card had gone through, but another customer saw what had really happened and shared it in a social media post declaring "This was one of the kindest things I've ever seen."

a helping hand

Two participants in the Boston marathon were greeted with rapturous applause from the watching crowds when they crossed the finish line. They had stopped to help a fellow runner finish the race, carrying him over the line when his legs had given way beneath him during the final stages of the 26-mile race.

kindness in the air

A young mother was flying with her baby for the first time when he started crying. "I was feeling really awkward," she says. "I kept giving whispered apologies to my fellow passengers. Then one of the flight attendants came over and held his arms out. He assured me everyone understood and not to worry, and then took the baby and bounced him up and down the aisles for most of the flight. I could have wept with relief!"

hearing help

A regular customer in a restaurant noticed his waitress was struggling to hear him and learnt that her hearing aid had broken. He left a $500 dollar tip so she could afford the repair.

real-life superhero

Birmingham in the UK has its very own superhero in the form of a young man who dresses up as spider-man and takes to the streets to feed the homeless. The anonymous kind crusader buys sandwiches and hands them out to those in need every night. He believes "we should treat everyone as we would a close friend."

a chain of kindness

Driving home one night, a man stopped at a fast food drive-thru, and, as he went to pay, was told it had already been paid for by the driver ahead, who had left money behind the till for the next customer. Delighted by this gesture, the man did the same and left money for the next customer. Even better, the worker told him that this had happened 26 times consecutively.

caring colleagues

Thoughtful co-workers came to the rescue when a woman had her purse stolen on the way to work. As well as buying her lunch and a bouquet of flowers to cheer her up, they organized a collection to replace the money she had lost. "I was so moved by their thoughtfulness," she said. "They turned a horrible day into a lovely one through their kind actions."

posting positivity

One mailman in Connecticut delivers more than just letters and parcels. Along with his usual deliveries he posts notes of positivity through random letterboxes in order to spread a little cheer. His uplifting messages include "You are a beautiful human being", "Have an awesome day!" and "Remember you can achieve anything you set your mind to."

sir Captain Tom's
100th birthday walk

British Army Officer Thomas Moore began to walk laps of his garden during the coronavirus pandemic to raise money for NHS Charities Together, with the goal of raising £1,000 by his 100th birthday. On the morning of his birthday he had raised over a staggering £30 million and had become a household name across the UK. His birthday was marked in a number of ways, including flypasts by the Royal Air Force and the British Army. The centenarian was also delighted to be awarded a knighthood for his fundraising efforts saying he had been "given an outstanding honour by the Queen."

wearing skirts in support

A group of pupils united to show support to a fellow 15-year-old student who wore a skirt to school instead of the standard school uniform for boys. When some other children teased him, a group of his classmates – boys and girls – all wore skirts too in a show of solidarity.

kindness pays

It was revealed that the winner of the single biggest lottery payout in US history, the $1.5 billion Mega Millions jackpot, won because of a simple act of kindness. The winner wishes to remain anonymous but the store in South Carolina where he purchased his lottery ticket revealed how he had allowed a fellow customer also buying lottery tickets to go ahead of him in the line. Officials reported how "A simple act of kindness led to an amazing outcome."

dinner
for one

One little girl's act of generosity towards a homeless man went viral when she was captured on camera handing her dinner over to a man outside the restaurant where she and her family were eating. Her father tells of how she felt bad for the man outside with no food. "That urge she had to help someone less fortunate than herself was so natural," he said. "I've never felt more proud of her."

cat napping

One grandpa managed to make himself useful whilst napping on a visit to a local pet sanctuary that specializes in rehabilitating and rehoming cats. A regular volunteer at the sanctuary, he turns up each day with a special brush to groom the cats. On one fortuitous day he fell asleep on one of the sofas with several cats cosying up to him. A photograph of the retired teacher napping with his feline friends went viral on social media and raised an impressive $40,000 in donations for the sanctuary.

a cashier's kindness

A mother took to social media to thank the cashier who helped her during a rather fraught shopping trip. As her autistic daughter had a meltdown in the supermarket, the cashier distracted her by suggesting they play a game of "shop". She then allowed the delighted girl to sit on her chair and scan through all of their items. "This lady decided to show my daughter kindness instead of judging her behaviour," said the grateful mother.

koala
rescue

In a heartwarming moment of kindness, heroic teens went on a mission on bushfire-ravaged Kangaroo Island to save koalas. They rescued several of the injured animals, loading them into their car and taking them to safety.

picking up the bill

A couple has taken to frequenting a local restaurant in their hometown most weekends. They seek out couples that look like they could use a helping hand and pick up the bill for them anonymously because they were once poor and understand how it feels to have to count every penny. With their relatively newfound wealth they wish to spread a little happiness among those who could use it.

a shelf-stacking samaritan

A supermarket shelf stacker has been praised for his thoughtful actions when he took the time to walk a 95-year-old pensioner home after noticing he was struggling with his shopping bags. A heartwarming picture of the pair was shared 300,000 times on Facebook.

free dry-cleaning

A highstreet dry-cleaning chain in the UK offers to dry-clean suits free of charge for the unemployed. This incredible gesture ensures that those heading to job interviews can look their best, even in tough times.

hairdresser to the homeless

Once his salon doors shut for the evening, one selfless hairdresser takes to the streets to offer haircuts for the homeless. He travels to different parts of town, and even to hospitals in order to give haircuts to homeless people, helping to improve the self-esteem of those who can feel isolated from mainstream society.

first-class kindness

A mother and her 10-month-old daughter were on the receiving end of a random act of kindness when a businessman gave up his first class airline seat for them. She was travelling with her premature baby and an oxygen tank when he saw her walking to the back of the plane. He suggested to a flight attendant that she might be more comfortable in first class and offered to swap seats. "Thank you doesn't cover it," the grateful mother declared. "We need more people like him in the world."

safe crossing

A driver on a busy highway noticed cars having to swerve to avoid an elderly lady walking home with her shopping. Instead of driving on by, he stopped, loaded her bags in the car and drove her two miles back to her home.

a sunny snack

One student remembers the sweet gift of ice cream from strangers on a sunny day. An older couple was leaving the supermarket she was passing, taking two ice creams out of a box to eat themselves. Then they handed her the third. "I didn't have a lot of spare cash for anything other than basic food at the time," she said, "which made the gesture even more memorable."

blanketed in love

An anonymous donor leaves warm blankets on park benches all over the city of Boston during the cold winters. He leaves notes with them that read: "If you are cold, without shelter, and looking for comfort, then these are for you. Enjoy, and know that you are loved."

a paid parking ticket

One woman who had been staying in hospital with her sick child returned to the car to discover she had been issued with a parking ticket. But when she opened the envelope on her windscreen, inside was a note that said "I saw you had a parking ticket and thought if you're in the hospital car park it's probably the last thing you need, so I paid it for you." The gesture had a big impact. "I burst into tears," said the woman. "I hadn't slept for three days, had just been to hell and back, and this little selfless act was a timely reminder that the world can be a beautiful place."

toy donation

One woman's act transformed a moment of misfortune into one of happiness when she bought a toyshop that was about to go bankrupt. As well as providing the former shop owners with much needed capital, she made good use of all the toys that had been due to be claimed by debt collectors and instead donated them all to children living in foster care.

plastic bag ban

An environmentally-aware group of Girl Scouts was the driving force behind the plastic bag ban in the city of Boston. The Girl Scouts collected signatures for a year in order to bring the issue to city council. Thanks to their hard work and perseverance a measure to ban single-use plastic bags at checkouts was passed.

music for
rescue dogs

A Broadway violinist has a novel way of helping rescue dogs. When he walks into an ASPCA animal shelter, he's not there to take the dogs for a walk; instead he takes out his violin and plays classical music to help soothe them. As he plays, the dogs, who have often suffered some form of abuse or mistreatment, happily curl up on their beds, quietly listening and watching him play.

coffee shop comfort

An employee recalls how her boss took her to a coffee shop to tell her that they wouldn't be renewing her contract. "A public dismissal felt so cruel," she said. "I was totally gutted and burst into tears when my boss left me there." Her distress didn't go unnoticed and a woman walked over and offered her a huge slice of cake.

running
rescue dogs

A school cross-country running group has come up with an idea to bring a little joy into the lives of rescue dogs from a local animal shelter – they take the dogs with them on some of their training runs. Each child is paired up with one of the pups and off they run. Their coach declared, "it's the most fun the kids have ever had training!"

one good turn

A quick-thinking 12-year-old girl sprang into action when eating out at a restaurant with her family one evening. Looking at a table across the room, she noticed that the grandma in a big family group was choking. She leapt up and performed the Heimlich manouvre that she'd just learnt on a first-aid course at school. "I was so impressed by her swift actions," said the grandma. "That one good turn saved my life."

notes to brighten a day

A 7-year-old girl and her grandad took it upon themselves to try and brighten people's days. The girl wrote little notes of positivity like "Smile it's a beautiful day" and gave them to random people she passed in the street. When asked why, she claimed, "because we all need to be kind to each other."

stitching scrubs

Armies of volunteers looking for ways to help during the coronavirus pandemic started stitching scrubs to donate to the NHS due to a shortage in supply. The North London "scrub hub" was founded by a TV costume producer, more used to making costumes for actors than medical professionals. Up and down the country similar hubs were set up, bringing together groups eager to help workers on the frontline.

feeding firefighters

Two firefighters were waiting in line at a fast food takeaway counter when the siren sounded on their truck so they had to leave. A couple that had just been served handed the firefighters their food so they wouldn't miss out, then joined the back of the queue. Their selfless act hadn't gone unnoticed – when they reached the front of the line the manager refused to take their money, saying their dinner was on the house.

sisterly love

When a boy was teased at school for being "weird", his 6-year-old sister stepped in explaining that he had autism. But wanting to do more to help her brother and others like him who don't fit the mould of being "normal", she wrote a letter to the head teacher, with some help from her mum, asking if she could talk about disability awareness in school. She wrote: "I want everybody to understand that some people are different, but that we should all be treated the same."

a birthday delivery

One kind binman wanted to mark a favourite customer's milestone birthday, so on her 100th birthday he surprised her with a cake. The video of his thoughtful gesture has been viewed millions of times on social media.

free
bread

For years, a bakery owner in Kazakhstan has been baking extra bread every morning to leave on a stand outside his shop. A sign reads: "If you can't afford bread, take it for free."

birthday money well spent

When a 10-year-old girl spotted charity workers feeding the homeless in her home city, she was inspired to do her bit to help, too. She asked her mum if she could spend her birthday money on food for the homeless. Her proud mother agreed and they spent the day on the streets handing out soup and hot drinks.

the power of hand-holding

A woman recalls the day she was having a panic attack in an airport. "I was terrified of flying," she said. "I didn't know how I was going to get on that plane." Then along came a fellow passenger who sat beside her and held her hand. "I can't tell you how much that small gesture helped me," she continued. "Once we had sat there for five minutes with her just holding my hand, I felt calm enough to board the plane."

a generous new boss

A college student walked 25 miles to get to his first day of work after his car broke down the night before. Called into his boss's office he thought he was going to get reprimanded for being late. Instead, his boss – having learnt about his new employee's journey in that morning – was so impressed with his dedication that he offered to buy him a car.

the volunteers of venice

Female rowers turned the city of Venice's famous canals into channels of caregiving during the coronavirus pandemic. The charitable group called Row Venice used gondolas to deliver groceries to elderly and vulnerable people isolating in the city.

free flowers

One drizzly day, a florist in New York City was surprised by a man who came along and bought her entire stock for several hundred dollars. But instead of walking away with the blooms, he asked the florist to hand them out to people in the city. So she spent the day gifting bunches of flowers to strangers. "The reactions I got were incredible," the florist said. "Who doesn't like receiving flowers? The smell, the colours, the beauty of them is an instant mood booster." Inspired by this man's actions, once a month she hands out flowers for free.

coffee
gesture

A man in Canada walked into a coffee shop and left $860 behind the counter for the next 500 customers. Coffee shop workers reported a buoyant mood all day as delighted customers were told they didn't have to pay for their orders.

an anonymous gift

A woman on the receiving end of a random act of kindness took to Facebook to try and track down the anonymous donor who left £100 under a napkin on her lap when she was napping on a train journey. Earlier she had been talking to her mother about how stressed she was about her finances, having got into debt during her final year at university.

spreading the magic

A couple of retired teachers made it their mission to bring a little magic to the children in their neighbourhood by turning a tree stump in their front drive into a fairy house, complete with spiral staircase, garden, and letterbox. Children post letters to the fairy and the couple responds to every one of them.

home for
unwanted pets

One retired animal lover has taken it upon himself to provide a home for "undesirable" pets. He visits his local animal shelter and fosters the old and sick animals so they can live out their days in comfort, being loved and treated in the way that all pets deserve.

a floral gift

When one couple had to postpone their wedding due to the coronavirus pandemic they decided to donate all of their flowers to nursing homes where residents were having to self-isolate and visitors weren't permitted. One resident talked about the joy the floral gift brought them: "The flowers are absolutely beautiful. They've brightened the place up and made us smile during these difficult days."

legacy of kindness

A resident of a UK village left three houses to the council when he died, with the stipulation that they were to be rented for a fixed three-year term by young families, with a rental price of £300 per calendar month – this was in an area where rents on this size house averaged well over £1000 a month.

teacher turned babysitter

A single mum student in the US quietly snuck into the back of a lecture hall hoping that nobody would notice she had brought her baby along, having been let down by her babysitter at the last minute. When her baby started crying she got up to leave but was promptly stopped by her 55-year-old lecturer who smiled, took the baby, jiggled her up and down to soothe her, then, using the mother's baby carrier, strapped the baby to her back where she remained happily for the duration of the lecture.

the spirit of christmas

One fateful January, a young boy's house was destroyed by fire. He lost all of his belongings, including his recent Christmas presents. A classmate asked if he could give the boy all of his presents to help make up for his loss. "I have enough already," the boy announced. His mother talks of how they rewrapped his presents and dropped them over to his friend, who was staying with grandparents. "His face was an absolute picture," she recalls. "I'm so proud of my awesome little boy."

An Hachette UK Company
www.hachette.co.uk

First published in 2020 by
Pyramid,
an imprint of Octopus
Publishing Group Ltd
Carmelite House
50 Victoria Embankment
London, EC4Y 0DZ
www.octopusbooks.co.uk

Distributed in the US by
Hachette Book Group
1290 Avenue of the Americas
4th and 5th Floors
New York, NY 10104

Distributed in Canada by
Canadian Manda Group
664 Annette St.
Toronto, Ontario,
Canada M6S 2C8

ISBN: 978-0-7537-3447-6

A CIP catalogue record for
this book is available from the
British Library

Printed and bound in China

10 9 8 7 6 5 4 3 2 1

Publisher: Lucy Pessell
Designer: Hannah Coughlin
Editor: Sarah Kennedy
Editorial Assistant: Emily
Martin
Production Manager: Peter
Hunt
Illustration: 123rf/Ernest
Akayeu
Icon: Created by Zoo Studios
from Noun Project